STRAY FROM LUST
STAY IN LOVE

Felicia Corbette

Copyright © 2017 Felicia Corbette

All rights reserved. No part(s) of this book may be reproduced, distributed or transmitted in any form, or by any means, or stored in a database or retrieval systems without prior expressed written permission of the author of this book.

ISBN: 978-1-5356-0983-8

STRAY FROM LUST
STAY IN LOVE

No longer a wish
Or to wish
I am writing every line to the story of You and I
This story will go on forever with new chapters of us
Beginning with believing
And to trust the words I hear
Pages of how faith comes
How deep this love could go
When you think with your brain you see a dead end
But with His mind, you hear the beginning, a new way
A new life

I

You are my Peace that I once feared.
A blissful Love that I strayed from
Still, I yearned for Your presence in the absence of my Faith
Now holding on to so much hope inside
Your word, so precious, that in your presence I blush
Filling Joy inside my heart
I take a breath belonging to our familiar Love
It was always here but trapped in doubt
For doubt was what I was always carrying in my mind
Yet, my familiar stranger
My Love and friend
I know you feel the Love I am afraid to show loosely
This tight grip on my heart is being released
For with your forgiveness, Love and patience
I am confidant
My courage that I want to hold and to have
I Love You pure
I Love You like a child, innocently
For You were always the One and for so long, I forgot

2

Lift me up in spirit when my heart is exposed to that familiar pain
Dry my eyes from the past so I can smile
I want to remain faithful
I want to remain loyal, available and teachable
Flat
Not able to feel the cracks in my heart that I have caused
Allow me to turn and not be capable to split, again
Mold me into the right
To leave my weakness
To leave my hate
To leave my doubt
Allow me to flow in Love resembling a waterway
With all Your Grace
No option do I desire to run any longer
Locked in to the identical situations I was imprisoned in before
However, I shall endure in Your way
To develop, to mature
Remove from me any thought of doubt that I cannot
For I can because I am
Love, that is pure and Kind
Ready to blossom
Ready to have the Joy

Consume me with Love
So inside can heal from anything that is not of
And carry You within me
Our God

3

Take a sit with Him
Faith will walk with you to that door, if it is what you choose
Through the cold and the hot
The rain and snow
Birds remain to soar above and sing their melodies
As my flesh sat upon a cold step
Feeling a shiver
My spirit warmed me
No longer thinking about the temperature, I settled
Right into whom I was becoming
And what I came to do was write
Embracing the breeze
No longer thinking about the images belonging to this world
No more feeling the cold for it was just a word
Hear what is beyond your sight
I did not feel what it was
I heard what was calling for me to do
Breathing in as my hands drift along
Forming words on each line
And another poem has been written

4

I weep
Warm heavy streams poured from these eyes
Not a thought to make me sad
Not a person to make me hurt
But I weep
Loud sobs and a few quiet cries
I spoke of being ready to let go of anything that was not of love
Overwhelmed when I realized I am
So I breathed
Deep breaths in through my nose I held so long and so strong
The more I breathed in
A curve to my lips began to form
And my voice projecting, I believe
Holding in that deep breathe a second longer
With more control than having control
I let it all go
Softly the breath left my mouth
And just as long as I breathed in was how long I breathed out
Blissful
I believe
I am

5

The Love that fills within me only overflows
To those around me, I rejoice
In what I feel and by what I hear
I want to spread that in which all can rejoice along
Basking in this light
A new life I choose
No longer to question but to only serve
The only thing I know how and know best
I am ready
I am Joyful
Like a child's first day of kindergarten
The beginning of this seed and now ready to be planted
I absorb the water that is being given and I shall grow
Tall in Grace
Strong in Faith
And beautiful as God
This kind garden
I bring patience in all walks
So I can receive all that I am
Ready to speak the words I hear
Here written
I am a writer

6

These were never words written for your soul
Your impairment hearing can only have you assuming you know, when darling
You are far from aware
Blinded by my spirit
So you're not hearing or seeing
Ignorant to Love
So let me give you some enlightenment
The pens I held in this dominant hand could only curve the letters to form words that created these verses
Poetry, my loudest voice
So, I ask for pardon when your notion about my
Quality of beauty and intensity of emotion
Gave you any thought concerning you
I was craving One Love only I could find within myself
Searching for who I am and needing my inner child more than ever
Possessing these thoughts that bled on paper, left a stain
That each page flipped was always there
Similar feelings written but always there
Nothing else to put in writing so yes
It always had to be about the Love I craved within myself
As if it were food to fill my hungry belly

Your disappointment that lingered on your course tongue was discouraging then but now I laugh
I was fooled by flesh
Thinking it was you I wanted when I only needed me
To Love myself again and to embrace all that I am
Pushing through doubt
I swing on that fear
And arrive in a place of self-love
Only to have my Father beside me
For He is my other half
The curve to my smile
The tone to my voice
The sparkle in my eye
The Joy in my laugh
The freedom in my spirit
The courage to be who I am

7

My love

He is

So rare to others

As a fruit that grows on an island

Only having a passport to reach

Then once you arrive you have to walk through the unknown

Surrounded by nature and the clearest of waters

Breathtaking views, however, all you can do is breathe it in

My love

So Kind

Gentle like a newborn baby resting in their sleep

With his soft touch that never comes with pain

He embraces me like a warm blanket

Never feeling cold

My love

He is true

Honest with every word and shown in all my doings

Trust what you hear and all will be revealed

My love

With so much to give yet always remaining filled

It flows within me and shines out to you

My love

8

Centering myself in the middle of an unknown space
Familiar faces now out for me to find, revealed
A blank mind and an open heart
All that I can really absorb at this moment
Breathe in deep and let go
Lifting my heart with acceptance
Feeling it rise like a balloon that gets caught by the wind
Soaring up and away above it all
Peaceful and mindful of who I am and not who I can be, right now
In this moment
I channel any feeling that is not of Love to cast away
Release from within me any part of that negativity, fear
Courageous of all who stands before me
I smile and remain all that I am
Love

9

I weep for the Joy inside my spirit
The acceptance of Love
Of God
Father
I am in awe of Your Faith Love Peace
You accept me
Not in just all that I am but all that I am not
I will praise You
Worship
Worship
The depth of that word
Worshiper, I am
Desire just Your Love
For it is all I need
Lifting my spirit high
Many times we fly together
Higher and higher
I can feel the grasp on my feet no longer
It is trust
It believes
It is Faith
You come and change my mind

The thoughts that possessed me are gone
Thought
Just a dead word
No images do I carry in Your mind
Just You
For it has always been You
The One
My Love
Flowing out like a stream that is swollen from the rain
You flow in and through
Down on my knees I weep for the Joy only You embed in my spirit
My heart pure
Oh Father
I never said Your name
I never called Your name
And You were always there
Patiently waiting
For You knew I would and already had
It was I
I strayed from Love and stayed in lust
The hush to my lips are now open
But with obedience
To speak when You say and do not speak when You say
For You are, that powerful
Wonderful
Amazing
Loving
Caring

Soothing
Above all
Our Father

10

I have felt the ground on my face pressed down
Only were my eyes able to move
But I still could not see my surroundings
Pitch black
My thoughts deafened me of only negativity
I could not hear my Father's voice
And I was without my lovely Mother
This was no garden
I was without every fruit
Far from beauty
Only the bare cruelty of the wilderness
It consumed my thoughts and tried to reach in my heart
The doubt was great but by heart kept close, a Peace
Pureness that pushed out the lust and fear and doubt
Knowing that this cannot be all
This was not Love
My weeping soul mourned for something that still lived
Unknown but knowing
There is something more

11

The spirit that speaks in all truth and glows in the beauty belonging to
Love
Blushing in each word said
My mind is at Peace to know all I need to do is worship
Loving that chosen word
How dramatic in awe
Worship
I shall
For He is the best
My Father and all will know
Our Father
My savior
He who brings Joy to all
Peace to my mind
I sway to the beat in my heart
Forever loved I am
Accepting
Basking
I breathe
Sometimes I weep
But these tears are all of Joy
Cleansing and clarifying

It's a joyful feeling to no longer have tears belonging to pain
I weep because I know
I am ready

12

The spirit who sings almighty
With a voice belonging to the strongest angel
To the highest volume I hear the Peace
No restrain from Your voice do You project
Drifting away all hate for Love of the Father to come in
She settles the body and brings ease
Joyfulness rooted into our hearts
With just a song
Just a voice
Just Your spirit
Your pureness
It is real and it is raw
Truth and trust
Such a lovely spirit
No eyes do I need to see
Hear the voice belonging to your fruit
Waking up souls and lifting spirits

13

I love the mirror I have before me
Bashful in the words of truth
Hopeful in the image it views
Love in which it reflects
So clearly on the inside that a blur is just a word as it rolls off the tongue
You are love and that is lovely
A glow so bright, I daze
Smiling
Oh how I have missed You
Just as innocent as I left You
I will carry You
Hold Your hand and never let go again, in fear
Hold your hand and never let go again, in lust
Then once you Love, the two will connect
Just
As
You
Are

14

Imprints on my heart
It keeps me in Love
Such an impact
Each sea word
Washes away the dead words
You are powerful
So believable
Truth and trust
I can change the world
With a Father like no other
Brethrens full of Faith
Overflowing with Love
Basking in Peace
We are One
Comforting the many
We are One
Guiding them to Your way
We are One

15

Perfection, maturity when you can hear
Now seeing all You were all along
My deepest apologies of who I used to be
Hopeful in You to see in me all that I am today
My inspiration and role model You have always been
Walking and believing
I run in trust
And will arrive by Faith
All that You are is a graceful beautiful masterpiece
A creation from the greatest and only Father
He has given you the highest power belonging to Love
A gift only wrapped for You
A mother's love, intuition and nurturer
You have kept me as a child
Innocent from everything that surrounded me
I never understood until now
So appreciative I am for that and for You
My child like behavior remains pure and now unleashed again
I hold my own hand because of You
Loving myself more than I could have ever imagined
Overflowing with only Love
I give back and still remain full

You are amazingly strong
So sweet I smack my lips to the image of Your being, your smile
Embedded in my heart and forever it will remain there
My mother, best friend and companion
All in one I have with You
Feeling strength in my back to hold me up
You have given me life with a Father I am proud to call upon when I need
For that reminder of who I am and who I was always meant to be
My mother's keeper
Never part again I shall from You
I hear You
I trust You
I Love You
The greatest gift of all is having You as my mother
And with all the hills and valleys we have climbed and went down in
Not being able to see past the slopes
We have arrived to the top
Reaching to the sun
Basking in the warmth of our Love
I create and give Love
Love to myself and to You
Joyful and blessed
So privileged I am to call You mommy
So thankful for your patience in me while I found myself again
Years
Years
Years

And I open my eyes again
With an image of a baby resting on the bosom of her Mother
The only clear image is of Your face looking down at mine
Safe and loved and all Yours

16

Sunshine filling into my life
A blush controlled by Love never stopping
Widening into a smile, I am
Accepting fully, myself
Growing at a pace that increases as I understand
As I accept
Who I am is Love
What I need is more
And as it flows within me and fills up to the tip of my toe and the crown of my head
I give
To myself and others
Weakened by life and circumstances
I change my view in which I see
Others observe and want to follow
I continue and enjoy my guidance
Strut as I talk and move as I walk
So soon will that be a statement in which I say out loud and no longer fantasize in the mind
I am and will be more
More than what you see
And more than I could possibly imagine

17

It's so selfish what you do
Over and over
Now I see it was for me to learn
To put it to a stop
I won't hurt again
I will not love you in my way
For I surrender
I craved for your love but it was only lust
I know now that you are not the One
You are two
Having so many ways, I should have known
Competing is for sports not for the spirit belonging to Love
You murdered a part of me
But still living was one Peace
Hope
You create families and abandon them
With your false and crooked ways
Lustful lies
But Love is true
Love is kind
It never ends or stops
It is forever
And it is what I choose

18

For Peace and a still mind you need to believe trust Faith
It brings Joy and Strength
I used to try and prove to myself that pain was a part of Love
Hard times was a part of life
Tears streaming in results of no change
The good would never last
My words were never understood
Desiring to just be still
No chaos
Carrying dark burdens instead of light
My journey was tiring and never a sure thing
Wrong choices always alternating in sadness, pain
Fear and doubt
Until I let it all go
Acceptance
For what it is
And it is not my battle
No longer insanity in this mind
Just Peace in His
Showing joyful smiles when I hear His glory
For He is the only One who can keep my mind pure and free
I believe trusts Faith

19

To a soul who I Love
Promises made but life destroyed them
Together we grew up spirit to spirit
Learning from this world in which we were born into
But our childlike spirits always kept us above
Never falling
And then maturing in lust we lost our Love
Allowing life's situations to take over pressured by time
Still with hope of you always being there and I the same
A friendship to the eyes of many appeared unbreakable
I held for so long
Our memories
Possessing the good as well as the bad
Flesh to flesh we disagreed
Spirit to spirit we laughed
And our souls mourned from its separation
Never having a chance for your clothes to be displayed in my store
A daydream we shared
Of a match made of you and I that others would adore
Time always reminding me of what we had
But as a child living in season
There lives no moment to worry or fret
When we were side by side

Only heard was laughter
Our days filled with surprises as well as joy
A path I took lead to our first goodbye
But instead it was only
"I'll be hearing you"
There is no such word as goodbye with you
Your spirit and soul
So lovely and kind
Free and inviting
Keep that shine from within that no soul
No word can take away
And though this path we have created
Belonging to this heavy and dark world
Where we are two souls who drifted away from a past time
But in this season I rest
Full of only Faith
That our souls will rekindle
A journey will begin
For me as well as for you
Belonging to this world
Where we are two souls from a past time

20

Writing became my sanity when I thought I was losing my mind
So many images belonging to this world would scamper about and I let them walk on paper
Pain consumed my mind
Becoming too familiar that I could not identify Joy
Anger rising as I would realize this was not my first time
I have been here before
Same wrong choices
Trying to push through that wall of doubt and fear
I believed that a Love that is true could perform miracles
A miracle so big that it will join us together all over again
Unknowing of who but knowing there lives, One
His story
It is forever and forever is where we belong as One
I craved for a true Love
But emptiness consumed my broken spirit
And tears began to spill, pouring out
Uncertain about who I am
And I feared
Not that I didn't know who I was but that I may never find out
To find a Love that you come across in just One being
One spirit

To have Love, joy, Peace
It is only You that I vision such a life
And I am living
Faith behavior

21

You are healthy for my soul
Vital to my spirit
Nourishing my heart back to its original condition
Before it was exposed to so much toxic,
Poison that crippled my mind
You have released from me all that I held in
The fear of doubt of who I am
A gift given and now you have shown me
Detached me from this shell and wiped me clean
Soft blows to who I was gone in the wind
Like dandelions but I did not wish
I prayed
And I shall always
Weight lifted off for me to stand tall
Both feet planted on the ground
Coolness beneath my feet as I grip my toes on the bright green grass
Breathing in, I reach my arms up above my head
My heart lifted and open
I am bold
To stand alone in this moment with only the presence of God
I am supported
Only capable of softening my soul the more hardships I endure
For that one sun ship

22

I choose Love
You fall short to see the big picture inside my frame
This heart of mine is bursting with color and life
Something I forgot to see while I was constantly the blame
Lessoning myself lower and lower into a guilty hole
I learned to rise from this dark burden that has been keeping me down
I accepted what was being given and let things happen
But I couldn't seem to release this One
Still with a desire and no other could come to comparison
Craft my mind, possess my heart or carry my soul
Only You
Having around me everything except Your Love
Tears of pain and loss
Not the body but the soul
Yet I continued to wait for a change I knew would come
Because a Love lost is always found
If that Love is true and together we are just
So I am waiting for You
Even if it is another life
We will come back as doves
Soar together
Become as One and fly away home

Now waking up to know I am loved
Those little things that I never have to say for You know me so well
We are molding a masterpiece
Letting our hearts be the artist
No doubt
Just Love

23

Because He touches my spirit
Brings me to my knees
It is the weakness, this flesh dying
And He gives strength to my soul and mind
I just weep tears of joy
I am worthy to our Father
His mercy
All I can do is praise Him
For He has saved me
He can save you
My savior
He has woke me up
Holding my hand and walking with me
No longer do I fear
I cannot
I am here to restore Faith on earth
Wake up and hear
The strong, angelic, assuring, righteousness belonging to the Love
belonging to God
Hear Him
He is for you
And with His love
It is the purest
The sweetest
Never ending Joy
My forever

24

I call on You and wait
If time comes to put pressure, You remind me that we live in season
For all I am to do is pause
Then pray
I have missed no one and no thing
For You are all that I need
My heart's true desire
My spirit is in awe of Your word
Your voice
How assuring in these crooked minds
I call on You and wait
For now You have exposed me
Of a fear I used to keep alive
My life consumed in a dead word
For that is all fear is
Fear has no place in His mind
No doors open for doubt
And the ones that are cannot be closed
I am Faith behavior
Forever choosing our Father
He is Love